How to Finish the Test When Your Pencil Breaks:

A Teacher faces Layoff, Unemployment and a Career Shift

By Cari Harris

A Publication of The Educator's Room, LLC
Atlanta, GA

How to Finish the Test When Your Pencil Breaks: A Teacher Faces Layoff,
Unemployment and a Career Shift
By Cari Harris

Copyeditor: Franchesca Lane Warren, Bossy Girl Communications, LLC.
Cover Design: Christina Jones, Visual Luxe Graphic Design Studio
Interior Design: Cari Harris
Title: Casimir Covert-Keefe and Cari Harris
Photography: Madeline Metcalf, Madeline Metcalf Photography

Published in the United States by The Educator's Room, LLC
(http://www.theeducatorsroom.com)
ISBN # 978-0615815145

Table of Contents

Acknowledgements

I would never have had the opportunity to write, edit, and publish except for the amazing Franchesca Warren, the Founder and Publisher of *The Educator's Room*. She not only provided the platform for me to express my thoughts, but she is a constant source of friendship, instruction, inspiration and encouragement to me.

Thanks to all who read and edited with the patience and tolerance only friends and family can display: Carson, Jordan, Shannon, Stephanie, Susan, Austin M., DG, and Fran. Thanks to Austin R., who taught me how to stay physically healthy throughout my journey. And to Connie, who taught me how to keep my mind healthy at the same time. Thanks to Bobby for always believing in my professional expertise. And thanks especially to the *Derek Zoolander Book Club for Kids who CAN Read Good!* – my constant source of laughter, fun, good books and conversation, cupcakes, and rejuvenation.

Thanks to my family for supporting me through these years of unemployment and struggle. I could not have made it this far without my parents, Susan and Jon, and my brother, Jon, and their unceasing generosity. And thanks especially to my son, Martin, who is the smartest 11 year-old I know, who makes me laugh in the moments I most need it, and for whom my sun rises.

And finally, thanks to my former school district for removing my position and the job that I loved so much. Being tossed out into the winds of uncertainty has brought me growth and change like nothing else could have. I wouldn't wish sudden unemployment on anyone, but I can finally say that losing my beloved classroom was not an end, but a beginning.

Author's Note

Most of the chapters in this book were originally written as columns in *The Educator's Room* as part of a series called "The Journey of An Unemployed Teacher." With some exceptions for style and flow, those chapters have not been altered from their original publication. They were written over the course of the first six months of the 2012-13 school year. The path taken over that time is reflective of the real-time changes and thought processes I experienced as I reflected on being an unemployed teacher.

As noted in the original columns, the thoughts and statements in this book belong to the author alone and do not represent the opinions or positions of *The Educator's Room*. Nor are they meant only for the eyes of those who are unemployed.

Hopefully, the path I walked (and continue to walk) can be helpful and encouraging to *all* educators, whether they are working in the classroom or not. The main goal of our collaborative effort at *The Educator's Room* is to inspire teachers to be confident in their own expertise and to find their own personal brand. This allows them the freedom to no longer be dependent on the whims of their district or school.

Building a professional path that veers from the traditional expectations of teachers can be a very scary prospect for educators. But now is the time to believe you have more to offer than only the position you fill in the classroom. We're all in this amazing, frustrating, passionate, soul-searching, exhausting and rewarding profession together!

For Martin:
we turned left!

Prologue

The Unemployed Teacher:
A School Year Begins Without Us

AUGUST 2012.

I TOOK IT FOR GRANTED. I took for granted that once I found my passion and had seven years experience under my belt, I was safe. My passion is teaching Social Studies – I especially love Civics and Sociology, but have taught everything from Global Studies to US History. I had developed and nurtured the first AP Government course in my school. I was the only Social Studies teacher in my department who could offer college credit for Government courses from the local community college. With a counselor colleague, I had designed a school-wide Peer Mediation program for which I trained and advised really dedicated students every year. I was the Vice President of my union! I took it for granted I would be there forever, safely ensconced in my classroom. But I wasn't safe. The old model of education no longer exists, and teachers can no longer be guaranteed to settle in for a smooth, 30-year career.

I knew the cuts were coming, and I knew I was likely to be affected. That didn't make it any easier when, in March 2011, I was called into the principal's office and told, with all due regret, that my position was cut. I don't even remember the rest of that day.... or even the rest of that week.

~~ * ~~

Our district was hit particularly hard. For years, we'd floated on a surplus of funding that many other districts never enjoyed. However, the school board did not plan well for hard times. Suddenly, as the economy collapsed, the surplus disappeared – and then we had a massive deficit. I live and work in Oregon, where we lack the third leg of the taxation stool: a sales tax. Oregon also voted in 1990 to limit property taxes and unlink all but $5 per $1000 of property tax from education. So now our education funding comes from the state's General Fund (which relies mostly on income tax) and... the Lottery. When the economy collapsed, Oregon shot up to over a 10% unemployment rate (thankfully, it has worked its way steadily down).

With skyrocketing unemployment, state revenue plunged. I probably had an extra year of work that I didn't realize at the time: the 2009 federal stimulus kept a lot of teachers working for an extra year. However, Congress chose not to renew that investment.

I, and 80+ teachers in my district, had to finish the last 3 months of the school year in 2011 knowing we would not return. The teachers who kept their jobs struggled with survivor's guilt and fear of what the next year would bring with so many of their colleagues gone. Our high school lost 35 teachers, and every elementary and middle school lost their librarians, along with teachers and assistants. Our high school social studies department lost three positions, and despite my seniority, I was that final, third position cut. In other departments, teachers of two or three years' experience kept their jobs. The arbitrariness of the cuts made the situation that much more surreal. I'm sure this story is familiar to many teachers: both those who find themselves in the same situation as me, and those who have survived Reductions in Force (RiFs) in the last few years.

In July 2012, the Hamilton Project[1] examined government data and found that 220,000 teaching jobs were cut between 2009 and 2011. The Bureau of Labor Statistics has reported that from June 2011 to June 2012, 130,000 more positions were cut.[2] Those positions are only the ones the Federal Government can track because they are state employees. The number of private school teachers who have lost their jobs because parents can no longer pay tuition is a number that is anecdotal at best (here in Oregon, several

[1] Looney, A., & Greenstone, M. (2012, August). "A Record Decline in Government Jobs: Implications for the Economy and America's Workforce." The Hamilton Project. Retrieved from http://www.hamiltonproject.org

[2] Waldron, T. (2012, August 3). America Has Hundreds Of Thousands Fewer Teachers Than It Had Three Years Ago. *Think Progress*. Retrieved from http://thinkprogress.org/economy/2012/08/03/635501/america-teachers-job-losses/?mobile=nc

small private schools have closed down completely). So we're talking about *over 350,000 professionals* who have suddenly found themselves not only separated from a career they pursued passionately, but are now also competing against each other for the few scraps left that crop up from time to time.

A significant aspect of this Great Recession is the *long-term* unemployment that has become pervasive throughout the country in the field of education. The reason for this is that so many of the positions that have been lost simply aren't coming back. In an era where school "reform" means increased pressure on educators, fewer and fewer teaching positions make the education environment even more tenuous for those who are still working. The chance of many positions returning is even smaller now. For those of us who are no longer teaching in a traditional school, there are so many more and new challenges that accompany the grief of not being in our classrooms when the school year begins.

This was the second start to a school year that I have experienced without being in a classroom since I lost my position. Dealing with job searches, temporary positions, substituting, unemployment insurance, life upheavals that come with a cessation of income, and the myriad of emotions that accompany the loss of a major part of my identity all appear here in this short volume. Perhaps my experience can encourage other unemployed teachers, or at least let them know they're not alone. And perhaps it can also give some hope for employed teachers who still feel tenuous in their professional security.

The main theme of this book is that those hundreds of thousands of teachers who are longing for, and working hard to return to their profession, their students, and to their passion, *are still educators*. Just because the lack of revenue in our states led to the removal of a position we formerly filled, it did not remove being an educator from our identity.

And that may be the biggest challenge of all for educators who have lost their positions: we don't *work* as teachers; **we are teachers**. Being unemployed does not take that away. It is what keeps us hopeful that perhaps next September, the school year will not begin without us.

"[Kids] don't remember what you try to teach them.
They remember what you are."

— Jim Henson,
It's Not Easy Being Green: And Other Things to Consider

CHAPTER 1

A Shock to the System:
How to Handle the Layoffs in Your School

AUGUST.

THERE HAVE BEEN OVER 350,000 TEACHING JOB LOSSES SINCE 2009.[3] Usually the story of education job cuts stops there. But what *really* happens inside the school or district once the decision to cut is made? Every state in the union has districts that have experienced a massive shock to their system through a Reduction in Force (RiF). Even when few positions are cut, it still causes loss and trauma.

---

[3] Waldron, T. (2012, August 3). America Has Hundreds Of Thousands Fewer Teachers Than It Had Three Years Ago. *Think Progress*. Retrieved from http://thinkprogress.org/economy/2012/08/03/635501/america-teachers-job-losses/?mobile=nc

When unions attempt to protect their teachers and students, they are painted as thugs and saboteurs of education. Those labels cause pain on top of the loss the teachers are experiencing. And teachers in districts without unions have almost no protections at all when it comes to job elimination. How do we deal with such a shock to the system?

In his book *Managing Transitions – Making the Most Out of Change*, William Bridges writes that it is usually not the *changes* that cause us problems, but the *transitions after the changes*.[4] Change is not the same as Transition. Change is often a situation or an event (a RiF or a layoff); transition is the psychological process that people must go through to come to terms with the change. Once the change happens in your school, everyone involved will go through their own transitions in their own time. It is thus very difficult to deal with trauma that is spread out over that many people who are closely confined together.

We are currently faced with a teaching profession suffused with a three-layered trauma:

1. Those who are suddenly unemployed facing the loss of their job and often the reverberating effects of that (losing health care, homes, families breaking up, etc.).

2. Those who are left to cope with overflowing classrooms, a lack of resources, more pressure from unfunded mandates and criticisms of teachers – all while trying to manage survivor's guilt and the loss of colleagues.

---

[4] Bridges, W. (2003). *Managing Transitions: Making the Most of Change* (2nd ed.). Cambridge, MA: Da Capo Press.

3. The always-present cloud of fear and suspense that threatens more imminent job losses.

That's a lot of trauma. Most districts are unprepared to deal with the psychological and emotional effect this kind of sudden shift in fortune can cause in an organization, much less an entire education system.

~~ * ~~

In our district, we learned several months before the hatchet dropped that we would be facing massive cuts, and it quickly became clear that the district might not have prepared enough helpful resources for our teachers. As a union, we decided we needed to provide what help we could. I drew on my background in Conflict Resolution and drafted several memos we sent to our teachers that provided important resources and tips as they faced the inevitable notices of job loss. As one of those teachers whose position was cut, I can say that no matter your role in your school, *being open and honest with the teachers you work with is the most valuable gift you can give them during this horrible process.*

Our union advised our teachers how to go about filing for unemployment insurance. We gave them detailed descriptions of how our recall list worked and what protections they had in their contract. We offered suggestions for options on job seeking and how to maintain basic health insurance. But mostly, we offered emotional support. If your district or school has faced this kind of trauma, or may face it soon, this cushion of acknowledgement and support can make all the difference.

A few of the practical issues I addressed for our teachers facing layoff:

- Why was MY job cut?
- What can I say when speaking with my Administrator?
- Is it okay to ask for a letter of recommendation or reference?
- Who else knows about my job loss?
- What if I burst into tears at my meeting with my administrator?
- Is there any point in writing down what is said in the meeting?
- What important things can I do after my meeting with the Administrator?"

Later I wrote, and the union distributed, a memo titled "How Do I Cope with This Transition?" This included a more personal conversation with our teachers, including topics such as:

- Am I normal? What are some common reactions to trauma or loss when change happens?
- Why am I feeling this way?
- What are practical ways I can manage my stress?

- I didn't lose my position, but I still feel guilty and sad. How do I cope with losing my friends?

- I know I wasn't laid off because of my performance, but I've lost confidence in myself as a professional, what do I do?

- Can I get professional help? How?

- Are there *any* positives left?

It really does help to have someone acknowledge what is happening.[5]

~~ * ~~

Often, when layoffs are suspected or announced - or even just feared - everyone goes silent. Teachers, used to fending for themselves and their students, go into survival mode, where they dare to hope for the best, but mentally prepare themselves for the worst. I think we can do more damage to each other by pretending we should just soldier on and that it will somehow get better.... or even, that we'll get used to it.

When I got that layoff notice, I needed my colleagues more than ever, and they needed me. I needed them to treat me just like we were finishing a normal school year together, and to not feel sorry for me or hug me every time we met in the halls. (Really, no one

---

[5] *The offered answers to these FAQs are included in Appendix 1 to this book*

wants to spend their free time outside of the classroom awkwardly avoiding pity!) My colleagues needed me to reassure them that I didn't hold it against them that they kept their jobs. We could do this for each other because we decided to be authentic about what was happening. By reaching out and confronting the uncertainty, we made it safe for all of us to be open with each other and not feel we needed to hide from the circumstances.

We are not the cause of the trauma we are experiencing through these difficult times. The shock to the education system is only the outer shell to a deep and ongoing painful transition that teachers are experiencing throughout the country, both personally and professionally. We're all in this together, so finding ways to cope together will be much better for us in the long run than pretending it's just not happening.

"TEACHING IS NOT A LOST ART, BUT THE REGARD FOR IT IS A LOST TRADITION."

— JACQUES BARZUN

CHAPTER 2

Why Do We Become Teachers?

SEPTEMBER.

LIKE THOUSANDS OF OTHER OUT-OF-WORK TEACHERS, I spend many hours a week looking and applying for jobs. The world of unemployment is filled with extremely relentless efforts that produce very regular rejections. Sometimes you hit a job opening at just the right time, and you have just the right qualifications, and this gets you to Step 2, or maybe even Step 3 of what ends up being a 40-step process. It's an employer's market, and so even the most highly qualified teachers face hoops that didn't exist in the industry even five years ago.

Every so often, I happen upon an application wherein I get the opportunity to respond in-depth to questions about my pedagogy and teaching style. My favorite question is: "Why did you become a teacher?" It is such a simple question, but it can be very difficult to answer. When we start teaching and get so caught up in the non-stop nature of planning, instructing, grading, caring, learning, (and of course, endless meetings), we often never actually stop to consider a cogent answer to this question.

Why did you become a teacher? Off the top of their heads, some teachers might respond with an enthusiastic "because I love kids!" or, "my subject is awesome!" or, "I grew up in a family of teachers and just always wanted to be one!" But what *really* drives us into this profession? We don't know when we first enter teaching how relentless the days will be, how endless the meetings are, and how constantly we will always have to work. We also don't know how incredibly invigorating it will be to participate in the stimulation of young minds, to introduce students to the challenge of critical thinking, and to learn more every day in the process of planning. But it is a *lot* of thankless work. Statistics tell us that almost half of teachers leave within 3-5 years of their first year. So why do I keep trying to get back into this profession?

When I first lost my position, all of the emotions connected with such a tremendous loss collided in me as I tried to figure out my next steps. I thought I might be one of the "lucky" ones because I had a previous career field to fall back on. "Reapplying skills" was all the rage when we were invited to attend a meeting about how the state employment office could help us transition. At that meeting, the employment advisor told a room full of recently laid off professional educators, most whom had masters degrees and years of experience, that there were tons of jobs in the *truck driving industry*, and that we simply had to "reapply" our skills! Yes! Convoy! ...I am not saying that driving a truck is not a noble profession. What I *am* saying is that the skills it takes to earn a graduate degree, teach for years and continue to be a passionate, dedicated educator might *distantly* translate to completely unrelated career fields, but there needs to be a realistic connection.

For the first few months after losing my position, I looked for teaching jobs and positions in the corporate and legal world where I'd worked before teaching. I'd been a paralegal and legal assistant for 15 years (which taught me that I didn't want to be a lawyer!). As a last resort, I figured I could return to that work. My progress toward education began four years before I started teaching. I'd had the privilege to work for a civil rights attorney in Northern Ireland, and eventually as a human rights activist and community organizer at the end of The Troubles there. It was during that experience, in the midst of a terrible conflict, that I discovered how deeply connected I was to the efforts of social justice and equity. It's also where I discovered how much I liked hanging out with young people!

I became a teacher because I found the "Perfect Storm" of life - I discovered I could combine my passion for social justice with my keen enjoyment of young people, all while pursuing my love of learning. That combination not only led me to teaching, but also guaranteed my long-term passion for the profession. I am an educator because I love my students and the possibilities they present. When I'm teaching, I love that I get to spend all day wrapped up in the very topics I would geek out about anyway! I love that I teach subjects that connect to the very events that are happening in the world, and that I can show my students the importance of their own lives and choices within the context of those events. I love that I get to learn new things every day. I became a teacher because it is who I am.

I have now refocused my job-hunting efforts back to the world of education. When I think about why I became a teacher, especially on the days when I'm just so tired of filling out applications, or not finding any job postings, I remember that my passion and my craft are not lost. I keep learning. I take the opportunity to have conversations and share knowledge every chance I get - and I keep looking. Everyone becomes a teacher for his or her own reasons. But once you discover that is who you are, there is next to nothing that can replace it in your heart.

> "I never teach my pupils, I only attempt to provide the conditions in which they can learn."
>
> — Albert Einstein

CHAPTER 3

Education Myths that Eliminate Good Teachers

OCTOBER.

TEACHERS ARE AMONG THE MANY CASUALTIES of this faltering economy, especially young, motivated teachers. So many promising educators – who have chosen a career path of little financial reward because they want to help growing young minds — are waiting in the wings, wondering when they'll get their opportunity. Those new teachers now must compete with teachers like me, who have been laid off because districts and schools can no longer afford to keep the number of teachers that would create a reasonable student-teacher ratio. With thousands of teachers per state laid off in the last few years, it is getting harder and harder to enter (or re-enter) the field.

Since the 2008 economic crash, the state revenue that districts rely on has dried up very quickly. But this in itself is a symptom of one of the major myths Americans often believe about education. Looking deeper into what we believe about education will give us more to consider when we think about the conditions both employed and unemployed teachers face in the U.S. The following are three major myths that affect the employment of good teachers.

Myth #1: Education is a Right

In fact, there is no Constitutional right to an education in the United States at the federal level. Though most democratic constitutions that are modeled after ours list education in their Bills of Rights, the U.S. has never constitutionally addressed the issue. What this means, at a very basic level, is that the federal government is not *required* to provide for the protection or preservation of education (specifically, there is no mandate to fund it). The Supreme Court verified this in 1973 in the case *San Antonio Independent School District v. Rodriguez* by ruling that there is not a "fundamental federal right" to an education under the Constitution. Therefore, there are wildly differing expenditures on education at local levels. In 2010, for example, Nevada spent about $8400 per student, while New York averaged $16,000 per student per year.[6] The federal government is under no obligation to mitigate inequalities in funding or conditions amongst the states and districts. Because of this, there

---

[6] *the Annie E. Casey Foundation Data Center as of 2010*

is no nationwide mandate to recruit or retain good teachers in the public education system, and no way to equalize funding (or pay) for all schools.

Myth #2: Standardized Testing and Achievement "Races" Improve Schools

In fact, these methods of pitting schools against other schools and teachers against each other work more as wars of attrition, where good teachers are eliminated in order to hire cheaper "facilitators" who can train students to take the standardized tests (as in Florida, for example).[7] The achievement focus of high stakes testing has only sped up the privatization of education.

New privatized and for-profit charter schools often don't hire teachers with as much experience or education as the public education system does. Thus, many teachers who find themselves without work equal to their qualifications also must compete in a field where many education opportunities are meant specifically for people without higher degrees or teacher training, and who are willing to accept lower than average wages.

High stakes testing has also served to drive many excellent and well-trained teachers out of the profession because they find they can no longer successfully teach because their classroom time is robbed by test prep and test taking. The new focus on "Race to the Top" and

[7] Hererra, L. (2011, January 7). In Florida, Virtual Classrooms With No Teachers. The New York Times.

other competition-based incentives for schools and states pits teachers against each other. These initiatives also set teachers up as the targets for states and districts that want to prove they are complying with business models of evaluations. Even as it gets harder for good teachers to enter (or re-enter) the profession, the teachers who remain are burdened more and more by issues that have nothing to do with the quality of their teaching.

Myth #3: Teachers are Paid Too Much

This of course is one of the greatest canards in the education debates – especially amongst those bent on breaking unions. Recently, *Mother Jones* Magazine compiled a list of average teacher pay across the country, and they found that it varies widely (again, due to the differences in local funding).[8] While there are many ways that unions can modernize and become more flexible (speaking as a former VP of my local – I am extremely pro-union, but I do know that the union model is one from a past century and could *definitely* be updated while still strongly advocating for teachers and students), it was unions that set the bar high enough that teachers at least make average professional salaries commensurate to their education and training.

One of the negotiations unions made early on was that teachers would accept lower professional wages in exchange for secured

---

[8] Gilson, D., Raja, T., & Lee, J. (2012, September 14). Map: How Much Do Your Local Teachers Earn? *Mother Jones*. Retrieved from http://www.motherjones.com/politics/2012/09/map-teachers-salaries-by-city

pensions, similar to other state workers and private pensions that were prevalent during the mid-20th century. But now those pensions are being robbed because states are unable or unwilling to fulfill their commitment to retired teachers. Consequently, due to the impact of the failing economy, teachers that intended to retire can no longer afford to do so.

Many GenX teachers, like myself, and now Millennial teachers, expected that Baby Boomer teachers would be retiring in droves by now, opening up opportunity for rising, eager and qualified teachers. But because that is now off the table for so many Baby Boomers who face a much more uncertain retirement than they expected, those jobs are still unavailable.

~~ * ~~

When we believe these myths, we create more layers through which we must wade in order to understand the nature of the problems in our profession. Instead, why not discuss how to value teachers more in order to create a profession that draws in and retains the most qualified and motivated educators around the country? Making equity across the country a priority, building up and supporting teachers rather than treating them as the enemy, and focusing on conditions in schools for students and teachers – *those* are the reforms that will truly improve our schools, make teaching what it was meant to be for employed teachers, and bring back those qualified teachers that are currently missing from classrooms.

"THERE ARE STORIES — LEGENDS, REALLY — OF THE "STEADY JOB." OLD-TIMERS GATHER GRADUATES AROUND THE FLICKERING LIGHT OF A COMPUTER MONITOR AND TELL STORIES OF HOW THE COMPANY USED TO BE, BACK WHEN A JOB WAS FOR LIFE, NOT JUST FOR THE BUSINESS CYCLE. ... THE GRADUATES SNICKER. A STEADY JOB! THEY'VE NEVER HEARD OF SUCH A THING."

— MAX BARRY, *COMPANY*

CHAPTER 4

Teachable Moments During Unemployment

OCTOBER.

AS TEACHERS, WE INSTINCTIVELY LOOK FOR THOSE teachable moments in the classroom. You know them – those moments when suddenly space and time open up to reveal an opportunity to take what is at hand and turn it into a way to delve more deeply into whatever subject we are teaching. Exercising this habit outside of the classroom is not so easy. I didn't find many teachable moments during the first six months of my unemployment. Mostly, I tried to cope with my feelings of loss, grief, fear, and insecurity. But as I have maneuvered my way through this unexpected turn in my professional and personal life, I've eventually managed to learn a few things. Here are some personal lessons that came along when I began recognizing those teachable moments:

Unemployment actually IS scary, so it's okay to be scared

Most GenXers like me began our professional lives fairly securely. There were jobs available after college, and even when some of us shifted and found new directions in our 30's, there was still ample opportunity. Most of us became adults after the recessions of the 1970s and early 1980s, so we did not experience too many massive economic disturbances once we began work. The effects of this current recession are far-reaching and long lasting – and we have no modern equivalent to judge its future path.

The unpredictability of whether jobs will ever come back, whether our career fields will be relevant within the next 20 years, or whether we will even have the chance to retire when we are older, all play into the scary atmosphere of being unemployed right now. There is evidence emerging that shows the longer we are unemployed, the less employable we are, and that is not something to fill us with confidence. So don't judge yourself if you're scared. I often am. But I'm no longer crippled by it, I'm doing my best to remember that courage is not the *absence* of fear, but the ability to face that fear honestly.

Hit the Gym and Talk to Someone

It sounds like a trite cliché to go to the gym when you've experienced a traumatic event – but it has done wonders for me. I always had good intentions about exercising, and for some periods in my life, I kept it up for a little while. But when I got laid off in 2011, I purposely joined the gym. For me, the membership was the only accountability I had that forced me to actually get out and go somewhere every day. Going to the gym got me out of the house, gave me time on my own, and actually helped me to start feeling better emotionally because I worked out my stress physically. I used a bit of my savings and a gift from a family member to also work with a trainer. Even while I tried to figure out my own direction in education, I learned new things about health and fitness from another educator.

The bonus of committing to a gym is you get into great shape! I've lost 3 sizes, learned how to run, and for the first time in my life, I ran a 5k! I can also bench press almost 85 pounds, and I am pretty proud of myself for that! The feeling of physical health and strength has done wonders for my mental and emotional life. And the challenge of continuing to work toward personal goals keeps me focused when I get distracted by the uncertainties of unemployment.

I also see a professional counselor regularly, and highly recommend this as well. Having an unbiased professional to talk with can make all the difference when working through difficult experiences. Friends and family may be there to act as listening ears, but someone with whom you don't have a personal relationship can be invaluable in helping you to explore possibilities for your life. In some communities, there is a stigma about talking with a counselor – but there is only strength to be gained in getting guidance from a professional. We expect parents and administrators to trust us and work with us because we are the experts in our field. When we face hard times, it's a good idea for us to trust the experts in fields that can help us. Both the gym and a therapist cost money – so when the savings start to run out, or you have no supplementary income, there are cost effective substitutes. I strongly encourage you to pursue them – they really do make a difference in day-to-day management during unemployment – and beyond.

Do Some Research and Make a Plan

Sometimes the best way to not feel crippled by the end of a path you thought would continue is to create a *new* big picture plan. I am a planner. I like to make my big and small goals, and then produce appropriate plans. My friends and colleagues probably wouldn't recognize me without the multiple sticky notes, calendars and lists that surround me. For me, my unemployment occurred within the same six months that my marriage ended and I lost my house to foreclosure. All of these changes resulted in my son and I having to leave our home and put all our possessions in storage. We've lived with family for almost two years now. These events combined at first to make me feel hopeless and without direction.

Slowly, I began looking for a new path. I learned how my state's unemployment insurance works (watch out: many states treat teachers differently because of the school year!). I began collecting links to job sites and making a schedule for myself on who I contact and when, so that I didn't repeat the same effort too often and get discouraged. **I highly recommend NOT doing a job search every day** – it can be disheartening, especially in the few months after the school year begins. Pace yourself.

Make several outlandish 5-year plans that incorporate all your best-case scenarios so your sense of hope can be nourished. But also make *realistic* 5-year plans so that you feel a sense of control over your own decisions and your finances. Think ahead as much as possible – being caught unawares was the worst part of being laid off.

Learning how to experiment with new plans has really helped me cope and be prepared for new eventualities.

Don't Lose Touch With Friends and Students

My first inclination after losing my position was to withdraw from the world. Sometimes, it's hard to face the sense of shame of not working in a society that bases self worth on employment. I can be hard not to be jealous of friends who are still teaching, and you also don't want to be the reminder of their own precarious situation. Whatever the reason, it's easy to find excuses to withdraw. Try not to do this.

Make an effort to reach out at least a couple of times a month to get coffee or go to happy hour with friends and professional colleagues. It really helps me to ground myself when I see my friends. It has also given me some closure to hear how things are moving on in the school without me, the struggles that my employed friends are dealing with inside the system, and the general frustrations of the job. Reminders that the grass isn't always greener help me to temper my feelings of separateness from my career field. I never wore rose-colored glasses about the education system when I was in it, but it's tempting to wear those glasses now that I'm on the outside.

My former students have also tremendously encouraged me. I keep in touch with many who graduated high school years ago, and I love those moments of joy and success when I see how they are progressing in their lives. Validating your belief in yourself as a skilled professional includes staying in touch with those who can reflect back to you that part of your identity. Even if it is hard at first, don't lose touch with what connects you to your passions.

Yes, sometimes I want to scream, "I don't WANT a teachable moment – I want to teach!" But most of the time now, I cope a lot better because I'm looking for ways to learn. Learning takes me outside myself, and that always helps me to focus on the possible, rather than the unknowable.

"In a completely rational
society, the best of us
would be teachers and the
rest of us would have to
settle for something else."

— Lee Iacocca

CHAPTER 5

Substituting:
The "Not-Quite-Teaching" of Teaching

NOVEMBER.

ONE OF THE NEW ADVENTURES I EMBARKED UPON AFTER MY LAYOFF was substitute teaching. Many unemployed teachers I've spoken to have substitute-taught for a very long time (sometimes half a decade or more), waiting to get back into a permanent position. Substituting can be one of the best – or worst – situations in which unemployed teachers can find themselves. The bonus, of course, is that you get to spend the day in a classroom and work with students. In order to do so, however, you will be a stranger (often in a strange school) and have none of the best parts of teaching (knowing your students, planning fun lessons, etc.). On the other hand, you don't have to grade work or stay after school for interminable meetings. There are definitely benefits and drawbacks.

My personal substituting experience was a challenge for me. I primarily subbed in the building where I taught high school, and from where I was laid off. At first, I thought this would be easier (and in many ways it was) because I am familiar with the workings of the school, the administrators and the other teachers. However, going back there to sub also felt like a stab in the heart, knowing that I no longer held a position there and was reduced to being a visitor. On several mornings, colleagues saw me coming in to sub, and asked me the same question: "who are *you* today?" It felt as if I had completely lost my own individual identity as a teacher, and now only served as a replacement robot in someone else's name.

~~ * ~~

The View from the Other Side.

As classroom teachers, we've all had our share of great – and horrible – experiences leaving our classes in the hands of substitutes. We get to know who our preferred subs are and which subs can handle which kinds of lessons. Some substitutes thrive on subbing and make a career – or a retirement – out of it. Most subs nowadays are either former full time teachers (like me), or new teachers who have matriculated out of their training, but have yet to find permanent positions.

It's not easy stepping into a class and managing students who often don't want you there or believe that they can manipulate you because you are a temporary inconvenience to them. Especially at the middle or high school level, you might encounter hundreds of students in your classroom during one day, and it is crucial to be able to manage the class in the way that meets the regular teacher's needs.

Now that I've seen substituting from the substitute side, I have found there are several things that a teacher can do to not only make the substitute feel more welcome in their classroom, but also make it easier to navigate through the day:

Have a Substitute Notebook or Folder.

If you take the bit of extra time it takes to make yourself a permanent notebook or folder to leave for substitute teachers, you won't have to do so much prep when the time comes that you need one. Handy items and tips to have in this notebook or folder can include:

- **A Directory:** Phone Numbers, Email Addresses, Instructions on how to contact Administrators/Counselors/Security

- **Basic Bell Schedules**: Your sub may be coming in on a special schedule day, so having the bell schedules available is handy. Another helpful hint would be where the sub should go for assemblies or rallies, or other events that may occur while they are there.

- **Names of the Teachers** in immediately surrounding classrooms (to ask for help).

- **Basic Operating Instructions:** for any mechanical, technological or other items (projectors, computers, document cameras, etc.) in your classroom (also – should blinds be closed/opened, chairs put on desks, etc.).

- **Emergency Procedures**: Where does your class go in the event of a fire drill, what are your procedures for a lock down/lock out?

- **Class Lists:** If you have an attendance system that allows you to print out class seating charts with pictures, this can be very helpful to a sub in identifying students.

- **Any notes on accommodations** or other issues the sub may encounter in a particular class. It's important that a sub know if they need to accommodate a student so that every student can experience continuity in their learning environment, despite not having their regular teacher there.

These are things that don't really change during a semester, so having them ready and prepared in a Sub Notebook can really help both you and the substitute. Even on those mornings when you wake up sick and have to make the last minute call to the school, knowing that notebook is accessible will give YOU more confidence that the sub will be able to manage your classes for you.

Leave as clear directions as possible in your lesson plan.

The management of a classroom can often simply boil down to a tight lesson. I know that it's hard to be prepared for anything, but if you have a few extra "emergency lesson plans" you can set aside that you can draw on for substitutes when you haven't had a chance to plan ahead, this can really help your classes move smoothly while you are away.

If you find a substitute who handles your classes well and teaches the lessons in the way you prefer, it doesn't hurt to establish a personal contact with them through email. Then if you need them, you can send a lesson plan directly to them, and they might even have time to prepare a bit for it. If your school's substitute system is not set up that way, having notes in your Sub Notebook will go a long way to making sure you come back to a class where you don't have to make up too much time after being gone.

Being a substitute can be very challenging, especially when you are a teacher that wants to be able to teach and work with students. Finding ways to welcome substitutes into the classroom, paving the way for them to manage students effectively, and giving them clear guidance on what is expected can really go a long way to aiding both the classroom teacher and the substitute in creating a successful environment for the students.

When a great many people are

unable to find work,

unemployment results.

-- Calvin Coolidge

CHAPTER 6

The School Zone: Keeping In Touch With the School Year

November.

The last third of the Fall Semester is that marvelous time of the school year when teachers begin to anticipate that (sometimes desperately) needed break coming in December. Some schools even get an entire week off for Thanksgiving (I was always so envious of that!). Often parent-teacher conferences happen around this time of year, and there are grading days to get those first report cards out. The best part about this time of year is that by now, teachers feel confident and at ease with their students because they know them all well.

All the names and faces are familiar, there are inside jokes, and comfortable familiarity accompanies the start of class. This time of year means the ability to adjust plans and teaching styles to meet the different needs and levels of students because teachers now know their classes more personally now. I remember how much I loved this time of year when I had my classroom because greeting my students had become positive and fun, I could gear my teaching style towards the different class personalities that had developed, I was much more confident in managing any issues with students. I also regularly got the "yo! Harris!" call in the hallways... or the solemn up-nod starting around this time of year.

It is an interesting sensation to mark the calendar by a school year pattern despite no longer working in a school. But this may be one of the most important things I do for myself as an unemployed teacher. At first, it was painful to be reminded of what I was not able to experience without a classroom. Indeed, the first autumn I was unemployed, I did not do this, and I absented myself from connection with the school year.

But now, that school calendar is a saving grace. The theme of this book is the idea that just because I don't have my own classroom right now, I am *still* a teacher. A mindful connection with the school year calendar now helps me to continue to nurture my teacher-self. I don't know if unemployed people in other professions do this, but as an educator who still hopes and intends to work within my profession, that rhythm of the school year is a way for me to stay in the "school zone."

Interestingly, unemployment does not necessarily mean boredom or lack of work (as can be the popular conception of it). Just looking for work can be incredibly time consuming. But as all unemployed people know, we can't fill *all* of our time with job searching because it can be very defeating to only focus on the hunt. So scheduling time out to do other professionally focused tasks really helps to compartmentalize the different aspects of unemployment. Time set aside for job searching has its place. But I also tune into the school year and engage in the profession of teaching.

I think through the subjects I teach and retool lessons with newer information. I research areas of inquiry that I haven't used recently or at all and incorporate them into original lessons. I am a constant learner myself, and so I do research and find ways to increase my awareness of tools and information pertinent to what I teach. This all engages my mind, connects me to one of the pieces I most love about teaching: the creativity. This practice also uses my time productively, and I get the very valuable sense of achievement that can often be missing during unemployment.

I also keep in tune with the school year through social networking. I had already set up a separate Facebook page specifically for staying in touch with my former students so that they could always come to me for advice or information. I make sure to stay in touch that way. I confess: I also use it to teach! Lessons and current events naturally form themselves on my newsfeed. Often we have fantastic discussions about what they are learning or experiencing. They are all now in college or graduate school, working or exploring, and all have moved into their adult lives. By staying connected to them, I get the wonderful opportunity to continue to teach and learn with them. They ask me questions or ask me to look at their work or engage me in conversation about issues in the news. Maintaining that connection taps into a part of my heart that loves that interaction with students and that back and forth of discovery and learning. We still get "aha" moments together, we still learn from each other, and teaching happens – in all directions.

The school zone can be risky because it *could* remind me of what I used to have and where I might be instead of where I am. The challenge of unemployment is not to live in the future or the past, but to find the richness of the present. Keeping in tune with the school year, continuing my best practices in creation of lesson plans and materials, improving my own skills in technology and research, and maintaining relationships that channel the best parts of teaching interactions, all combine to enrich my life outside the classroom and remind me of who I am. I'm an educator, so I might as well act like one!

"The calling of the teacher. There is no craft more privileged. To awaken in another human being powers, dreams beyond one's own; to induce in others a love for that which one loves; to make of one's inward present their future; that is a threefold adventure like no other."

— George Steiner, *Lessons of the Masters*

CHAPTER 7

Education is Changing and We Must be Ready: An Exercise in Self-Evaluation & Moving Forward

DECEMBER.

AS A TEACHER WHO HAS BEEN OUT OF WORK for almost two years, I find the holidays bring an interesting sense of out-of-sync timing. I can clearly remember the visceral relief at the arrival of winter break – it's so well deserved by the time it rolls around! All of my teacher friends are finally able to prepare for (and enjoy) the holidays and can't wait not to go into the classroom for a few weeks. For me, I'm away from a brick and mortar classroom all the time, so on the one hand, I've had a more relaxed time to prepare for the holidays, but on the other hand – I don't have a classroom. It's bittersweet for sure.

Last holiday season, I still deeply felt the loss of my position, and so I felt a bit more down. This year, I am starting to match the reality of the teaching job market (not that there is much of one) to the possibility I may need to be more creative in finding ways to continue following my passion as an educator. I'm going to use *this* holiday to open new pathways for myself.

The winter break can often be busy with holiday preparations, enjoying time with family, and (for quite a few teachers) catching up on grading and planning for the inevitable return to school. If teachers make an effort to find a few moments for themselves during the break, it is to perhaps sleep a bit longer, catch up on personal errands, finish a project or two – or maybe just watch a movie or read a book, if they are lucky. Rarely do we as educators take the time to consider where we are as a person or a professional.

Ever since the country began mandating a free, universal education for children, teaching has traditionally been a very secure career field. Up until a few years ago, teachers could find a position where they felt they fit, where they could connect with the students, and where they could stay...sometimes for 30 years or more. But that isn't the case anymore. With over 300,000 American teachers laid off or out of work since 2008, this career field is vastly changing. Even teachers who have jobs don't feel the same security. Charter schools can close at a moment's notice, states announce lower budgets every year, districts have to prepare for another round of layoffs, and schools are more crowded and exhausting each year. So now may be the time for us as educators to evaluate not only where we are professionally, but also what might be around the corner for us – even if it isn't in a traditional brick and mortar classroom.

~~ * ~~

The holidays and the New Year are always good opportunities to evaluate the year past, and sometimes we even make an effort to make resolutions. But any break in the normal routine during the year can be a time to do some fresh thinking. Resolutions can be made at any time and can be as simple as a list of books we want to read, or a new skill we'd like to learn. Sometimes it's a matter of thinking about how classes have gone so far this school year and making a list of some ideas you have for altering your curriculum, reading new research, or trying some new ideas for assessments or projects.

Rarely do teachers take the time to really think through who they are and where they want to go professionally. We don't usually have *time* for that kind of introspection! But if we don't take the time to imagine ourselves outside of our usual habits, plans and surroundings, we can be caught unawares if our professional life becomes uncertain. Because our career field does not practice a model of preparing the experts to be professionally flexible, teachers often have no way to envision advancing in a career field that often remains static for many years.

~~ * ~~

If you are one of my fellow unemployed or underemployed teachers, the following exercise could be a helpful way for you to begin to open yourself to new possibilities, or just see yourself in a bigger picture. If you are one of my employed educator peers, this might just help give you a boost, change your perspective a little, and even add a sense of security that you can prepare for whatever may be down the road for you.

The following open-ended descriptions are a start to creating a vision of who you are and where you want to go. Take a few moments and sit with these questions, and try to answer them:

My greatest strength as a teacher is...

My greatest strength as a friend is...

My greatest strength as a spouse/partner/parent/single person is...

Something I consistently avoid is....

I look for _____ to excite me

I am passionate about...

I am saddened by...

Something that outrages me is....

I read _____ for comfort.

I feel empowered by...

I am most proud of myself for...

I am a person who....

I never want to...

I will always...

The things that bore me are...

I want to impact the world by....

I am touched by...

I am...

I was...

I will be...

I would like to...

I was happiest when...

I long for...

My dreams used to be...

My dreams have changed/not changed because...

My hopes for the world are...

~~ * ~~

These aren't easy self-descriptors. But these aren't easy times for educators. As this New Year dawns, I find that the more open I am to examining who I am as a person, the more willing I am to walk through doors that may open for me professionally. The more I'm willing, the more the doors are opening. In the last couple of months, I've had new opportunities present themselves, a small thing here and there, but ways to stay in touch with education outside of a traditional school.

Even if I don't make it back into a brick and mortar classroom any time soon... or ever... I've begun to realize that there are infinite ways I can continue to pursue my passion for teaching, learning and working with students. And if I *do* go back into a classroom, I will be ever more thankful that these moments of reflection and consideration will make me an even better educator and professional.

I wish you excellent and restful breaks if you are teaching. If you are not working, I wish you a fresh new look at the pursuit of your dream to be an educator. Education is changing, and we must change too. Knowing who we are and where we want to go is the first step.

> "You will find that it is necessary to let things go; simply for the reason that they are heavy. So let them go, let go of them. I tie no weights to my ankles."
>
> -- C. JoyBell C.

CHAPTER 8

New Directions: Teaching in the Future and Finding a Personal Brand

JANUARY.

I SPENT MOST OF THE FIRST YEAR AFTER MY LAYOFF just wanting to go back. Back to the job I had so passionately loved. Back to the routine that was so familiar. Back to the students with whom I felt so at home. Back to the career that had been moving along at a sedate but solid pace. I just wanted to go back. I found a temporary position that first year, which assuaged my longing for the classroom. It was a challenging position for me, and I grew from it. But it was temporary and ended with the school year. At the start of the second school year as an unemployed teacher, my perspective began to change.

As previously mentioned, I took several substituting jobs in the first few months of this school year. The jobs were at my old school – the place where I'd felt so at home for the better part of a decade. But the subbing was disheartening. In a building where I had invested so much of my time, energy and passion, I got double takes and confused looks from people who thought they recognized me but didn't quite remember from where. The difficulty of being back in the halls that no longer welcomed me was an important step for me: I needed to get past the point of wanting to go back so that I could finally go forward.

Finally, 18 months after my layoff, I found the closure I needed so I could open a new chapter in my life as an educator. For me, the closure was a two-step process. First, the subbing at my old school helped me close the door on wanting to go backwards. Second, my continued search for a teaching position with no results (not because I wasn't hired, but because there are simply no positions open in my field) allowed me to finally understand that perhaps I could look beyond finding a traditional classroom position in order to continue as an educator.

What I discovered during this process was that the more I welcomed change and began thinking of myself as a professional in a new way, the more doors began opening for me. In late September, I began writing for *The Educator's Room*, which brought opportunities and relationships that have already helped me to grow professionally, and have given me courage on my new path. Near the end of the calendar year, I was offered contract work as an online teacher, which allows me continued interaction with students, curriculum and new technology skills. From there, I began the challenge of writing dynamic online curriculum as well. I have almost completed my thesis, and will earn my second master's degree this year. It is one more way to pursue new avenues for education, like teaching at a local community college or other institution. Pieces of the puzzle of how I will make a new living - but still continue as an educator - have begun to fall into place.

I also began exploring my areas of professional expertise. As Franchesca Warren asks, "What's your brand? If you suddenly no longer have a job, what will you do with that brand?"[9] The steps to discovering a personal or professional brand include determining your area of expertise, deciding what your brand stands for, strategizing about marketing your brand, and operating as an expert and building your portfolio.

This can be a seismic shift in thinking for many teachers. By its very nature, teaching follows a very traditional, comfortable career model that doesn't require much contemplation of individual marketing and individual branding. But with the sea change in job security in the education field, that comfortable model has disappeared for many teachers. I had to do a lot of internal work to find my own personal brand and the areas of expertise I wanted to pursue.

I discovered that while part of my teaching philosophy includes student choice and student ownership of the learning process, I had

---

[9] Warren, F. (2013, January 7). Teacher Branding 101: What's Your Brand? *The Educator's Room*. Retrieved from http://theeducatorsroom.com/2013/01/teacher-branding-101-whats-your-brand/

been struggling against a system that did not encourage those things. Once I was outside the system, I looked for ways to continue to be an expert teacher in the field I love (upper level social sciences), even without a classroom. I can be more than a tutor – I am licensed in multiple states, will soon have two masters' degrees, and have long-term experience as a highly qualified teacher. And so are a lot of out-of-work teachers. How can we take these skills and apply them to a changing world of education?

As I researched and contemplated the answer to this question, I was inspired by the new field of concierge physicians. A concierge physician is a doctor that provides private healthcare on a fee-for-service basis. Why couldn't teachers provide the same services? There are so many students, especially older students, who are individualizing their education now. Whether through online courses, homeschooling, taking college courses while still enrolled in high school, or just trying to work their way through a system that often doesn't meet their educational needs, today's students have a lot more options. A concierge teacher, similar to a concierge physician, could make house calls to teach curriculum to individuals or small groups. But there is more versatility available for teachers than doctors because personalized curriculum can be shaped for students using online communication as well as face-to-face teaching. With a licensed, trained teacher, the student can be assured of meeting state standards and/or being properly prepared for a necessary exam.

I was also inspired by *The Educator's Room* writer Paula Kay Glass, who left traditional education to start her own school and has been doing so for almost a decade.[10] There are also emerging opportunities in online teaching and small group learning. I realized that my thinking truly had changed because I no longer wanted to be the teacher of my past, but a teacher for the future. Flexibility, technology skills, comfort with student choice/student-led learning are the best parts of the future of education.

There are exceptional teachers in every school district in this country, and thank goodness for that. The school system only remains intact because of the dedication of the teachers who have continued to make it work, despite lowering budgets, lack of resources, and hostility towards educators. But there are also exceptional teachers who are now outside the schools because of the *same* lower budgets, lack of resources and hostility towards educators. That latter group of teachers, including me, must find a new way to teach or leave the profession they love in order to make a living. For now, I'm still not willing to leave the profession I love – so finding a new way to be an educator is my way forward.

---

[10] Glass, P. K. (2012, December 13). A Dream Followed: 5 Burning Questions About Running Your Own School. *The Educator's Room*. Retrieved from http://theeducatorsroom.com/2012/12/a-dream-followed-5-burning-questions-about-running-your-own-school/

The teacher who is indeed wise does not bid you to enter the house of his wisdom but rather leads you to the threshold of your mind.

—Khalil Gibran

CHAPTER 9

Taking Charge of Our Profession

Spring.

Like all teachers around the country, I am saddened by the stories of administrators and teachers around the country indicted for cheating on state standardized tests. It's disheartening, embarrassing, and maddening to once again see that the legacy of recent education policy is another negative portrayal of educators. At what point did teachers become caricatures that are either beleaguered, exhausted public employees or abusive, cheating, thieves of public money? Intellectually, we know that all educators can't be painted with a broad brush, judged by the actions of a few, or even claim mass victimization. People outside of education have taken over reform and policy, advising lawmakers and media, and building a false adversarial story that pits teachers against the rest of America. How did this happen? How did expert educators allow an incursion of non-experts to tell us what to do? In reality, we may have ceded our career field to outsiders because we have not taken charge of our own professional futures.

In this two-part exploration, I intend to delve into the not-so-popular topic of incentives and professional advancement. I very strongly believe that teachers are the experts in the field of education and should not only be treated that way – we should treat ourselves that way.

It is still widely accepted that education is a field one enters in large part because it provides a sense of *safety* and *security*. A teacher could settle into a classroom, do their thing, and 30 years later... voila! They are done! The problem with this model, just like the old manufacturing/industrial model, is that it cannot adjust to the vast changes in society, the economy, technology and education itself. We bristle at the idea of merit-based pay because for a century, education has been a completely longevity-based system. The longer you are in, the more you get paid, and the more job security you have. Even among civil servant jobs, the lack of professional incentive in education is remarkable.

But that doesn't matter, because, obviously: *teachers aren't in it for the pay!* But that pedantic response does not address the reality that we have not considered ourselves, nor have we *treated* ourselves, like the professionals we are. Professionals in medicine, business, law, finance, and even government must prove themselves to be the experts they are in order to increase their viability in, and their value to, their field. They are motivated to do so because they want to reach for that next level of professionalism and expertise that awaits them. And each new level provides new incentive: sometimes pay, sometimes leadership or certification or other professional advancement. However, teachers have had no such incentive mechanism built in to our profession. Possibly, it is because society still assigns teachers a mythical ability to survive and thrive on love for children alone (and we buy into that), or possibly because we teachers do not have a solid professional advancement model from which to work.

When I entered education in 2004, I had already spent almost 15 years in the legal field. During those years, I had to prove myself an expert in my field, and that I was exceptional at my job in order to move up to a new level of challenge and position (and pay). When I was evaluated by my superiors, my achievement was based on whether I had completed tasks, gone above and beyond what was expected of me, taken initiative, used innovation to accomplish my goals, collaborated successfully and shown consistent leadership. Demonstrating my consistently improved skills in research, client communication, organization and legal writing was also part of the process that determined whether I would be promoted and have more professional opportunities open to me. But when I became a teacher, there was no set system of moving forward as a professional. If I was going to challenge myself, I had to find ways to do it myself, usually within the small sphere of my own classroom, or perhaps via extra curricular involvement. There was no program to mentor me to reach for new levels of professional achievement.

Though every so often we had initiatives that involved mentoring, like most districts, mine didn't make this an ongoing model for all of the educators. All around this country, most teachers are content to do what they have been doing for decades, and many administrators are preoccupied with student discipline and raising test scores, rather than teacher development.

In the end, the bottom line of how I was judged as a professional amounted to the number of years I'd been on the job. What *didn't* matter: my skills, best practices, successes of my students, or contributions to my field. This was made painfully clear to me when our district experienced a massive reduction in force. Despite the fact that I had written & developed an entire AP course, had pursued professional development opportunities and been awarded a very competitive fellowship, was a leader in my union, had developed and sustained a successful peer mediation program, among other extra curricular involvement, I lost my position simply because I had fewer years in than the other teachers in my department. The same thing happened to many other teachers in my district. A colleague and friend of mine: an AP teacher who also ran the entire yearbook program and had successfully achieved an exclusive grant to bring Shakespeare Theater into the school, among many other achievements, lost her position because of the amount of years she'd been employed. Other teachers were transferred to positions they were technically "endorsed" for on their teaching certificate, but for which they had no training or experience. So expert teachers in those areas were removed to make room for others who were experts in entirely different areas. The examples of this sad waste of expertise, talent and energy in our field are endless. Clearly, this is not what is best for our students.

There needs to be a new system in place in which to measure our professional success, advancement, and value to our schools and districts. If a teacher has been in the field for 20 years, why must we assume they are better at their job than the teacher who has been in 10 years... or 5 years? On the other hand, if they are excellent at their job, then there should be no difficulty in demonstrating that and securing that position of seniority based on a clear record of skill, talent, successes and other areas of professional expertise.

The sad fact is that any efforts in which teachers have successfully collectively bargained for the benefits their positions deserve have also allowed the wrong kinds of protections to be put in place. Thus, even the most protective contracts can perpetuate a sedentary profession where there is no incentive to increase in experience, skills and professional successes. In areas where there is no collective bargaining, there are no protections at all. And suddenly, we are surprised to find that our state and national governments think it best to judge us on our student's performance on standardized tests. A solid professional advancement model from the beginning could have instantly made that alternative as obsolete as it should be.

We are experts, we deserve to obtain advancement, professional respect, and recognition in a field that is as competitive and focused on excellence as any other career field. Yes, it's a risk to add incentive, advancement and career options to a field that has enjoyed security in stasis. But that security is no longer there. It's time we, as individual professionals, and as a career field, stop settling for *Safe* and start striving for *Superior*.

~~ * ~~

Highly skilled educators who have been in the field for many years are now publicly resigning with harsh words for the changes that have taken over education. But the hard truth is we allowed ourselves to become inert professionals. It is easy to bristle at this suggestion, but the reality is, we didn't push our administrators or our legislators to set up systems of more accurate evaluations, or create new and innovative incentives to increase our professional experience. We didn't invite deeper scrutiny or ask for formal challenges to allow us to improve our expertise. As a profession, we stayed safe, content to collect years on the job, and allow that to be the only testament of success and security in our field. So the policy-making moved on without us – and now it is trying to roll over us.

We wonder why the American public doesn't respect us, or the work we do for their children. We wonder why teacher-bashing has become the new pastime, and when it will end. Some of us fall prey to cheating to grab hold of the false incentives offered by the false experts and false reformers. Some of us end up completely on the outside, laid off in purges that are the result of more restrictions on resources, or resigning because we can't take what teaching has become. Some of us live in constant fear about whether we will be able to return next year to the safety of our classroom. And some of us are so exhausted from the pressure, the mandates, the negativity, and the indignities that we aren't sure how we will make it to the end of *this* year.

As overworked as we may be, we must be more than what we have been until now. We need to see ourselves in the context of a career field that should have just as rigorous requirements for advancement as every other respected career field. And there *should* be advancement opportunities and authentic methods of evaluation. We *should* have to show our skills and expertise and be able to strive for promotions and other incentives. Why not? We must begin to refashion American education based on what *we* know to be the best practices, because *we* are the experts. Our students will only benefit when we are part of a system that encourages, rather than threatens, high quality educators.

Here are just a few ideas about how we might begin to remodel our profession:

Open Access & Peer Evaluation.
The time of closed classroom doors and teachers operating in total privacy are gone. Just the advent of flipped classrooms alone has turned teaching into a public, technologically accessible practice.[11] Some schools have already begun instituting a motivating program of open classrooms, and peer observations and peer

---

[11] *A flipped classroom is one that turns the traditional model of teaching on its head: students learn basic knowledge through video lectures or webinars, then classroom time is used for follow-up and hands-on work. For a great guide to flipping your classroom, check out Jonathan Bergmann's and Aaron Sams' book,* Flip Your Classroom.

reviews. A rigorous method of peer evaluation could be part of incentivizing the profession. In addition to more robust administrator evaluations, instituting a system for teachers to observe colleagues and provide anonymous evaluations (using a well-structured, research-based observation rubric) can give teachers the opportunity to receive valuable commentary on best practices. Such a system would allow each teacher to receive a number of anonymous evaluations to use each semester to inform their best practices. These evaluations can be part of a professional portfolio that feeds into formal evaluations as well. Yes, it takes extra time to spend 15 or 20 minutes in several other classrooms a semester, but the benefits of giving and receiving professional advice and learning from our colleagues can only improve our expertise.

Professional Portfolios.

We educators make extremely forceful, cogent, and well-researched arguments about the benefits of portfolio and project-based evaluations rather than high-stakes standardized tests for our students. Setting the example ourselves would be an important way to show the invalidity of using those same tests to evaluate teachers. Having a process (again, one with a research-based rubric) by which teachers can build yearly, electronic portfolios of their professional practices can add to the evidence that shows they deserve advancement and can serve as additional substance to observation evaluations. Portfolios can include unit plans with standards and content connections, along with pedagogical explanations; classroom management plans; student interactions and work; data collection on longitudinal student assessments; professional development or publishing; colleague collaboration; leadership experiences; use of technology and new pedagogical, content or management skills. Keeping a professional portfolio like this can also be a huge advantage personally for educators. Much like how important it is to keep your resume updated, electronic professional portfolios would help any educator be prepared in the event of a change in position.

Tiers of Advancement.

While yearly pay increases are common in most career fields, there are other ways to provide incentive for advancement. If several different tiers were installed into an educator's career path, there might be periodic ways to incentivize new skills, best practices and contribution to the field – perhaps three or four different tiers of mastery that become available every few years. There doesn't necessarily need to be a monetary benefit attached (though those are always appreciated). There are all kinds of other benefits intensely valued by veteran teachers: flexible time, resources to pursue further certifications or degrees, sabbatical opportunities, leadership positions, or the opportunity to provide professional development to colleagues, are among many ideas for this kind of advancement.

Advocacy Training.

In the end, public education is still... public. Hopefully, in a democracy intent on maintaining its liberty, a robust education system will remain a priority (though it's looking pretty bleak right now). We must become the most often heard advocates for our profession, not those of the private interests hoping to cash in on the dismantling of a free, universal education for all Americans. That means we should make it part of our professional training and activities to lobby, engage personally with lawmakers, and organize and participate in community activities that bring the relevancy of our industry into the reality of our neighbors. The voices of actual teachers are far more valuable than those of professional lobbyists or private groups with other agendas, and it should be part of our job description to know how to advocate for our profession, our students and ourselves.

We must not be caught like we have been in the last couple of decades: behind the times and tossed about by the winds of change. We must take charge of our own field. We must draw in our community and create allies out of our local citizens. We must be in constant communication with school and district administrators, and the conversation should go both ways, where educators have serious input into policy and decisions. We must actively and consistently advocate for ourselves and for our profession. Doing these things will lead naturally to the best, most advanced education and opportunities for our students.

Many teachers already have these skills and experiences, and can lead the way to a new model for our profession. We have to be more than simply present in our classrooms. We have to think outside the classroom. Yes, it will take more energy. Yes, we will have to transform the way we operate. And yes, that means we will have to do more than just teach. But in the end, it should be us, the expert educators, who decide our destiny as a profession. We must be the ones who make our career field essential to the progress and prosperity of our nation. We need to be the ones out in front of policy making. And the cold, hard truth is that we will have to work harder - and outside of our classrooms - in order to do that. But if there is anything possible amidst all the oscillations taking place in education, it is that we teachers can be the leaders of more positive change. We are the ones who know best what to do. It's time we do it.

It may be hard for an egg to turn into a bird: it would be a jolly sight harder for it to learn to fly while remaining an egg. We are like eggs at present. And you cannot go on indefinitely being just an ordinary, decent egg. We must be hatched or go bad.

-C.S. Lewis

CHAPTER 10

Finishing the Test

I HAD A VERY WEIRD DREAM ONE NIGHT AS I CONCLUDED WRITING THIS BOOK. In the dream, I was driving a very small car up a very steep hill. For some reason pushing on the gas pedal was more like trying to bicycle up the hill, it took that much effort. Suddenly and inexplicably, the left side of the steering wheel somehow popped off and the wheel was only attached on the right side. So (in the way of dreams) it was sort of flopping around in my hands. For some reason (in the way of dreams) the detachment of the side of the steering wheel caused the car to start sliding backwards down the hill. As I tried to get the car to go forward up the hill I got more and more frustrated. Then, out of nowhere, a big truck with a giant silver grill was behind me. My car slid backward into the grill, and as soon as it hit, the giant truck started pushing me back up the hill. But it did not seem like it actually *meant* to help me. So because my steering wheel was still wonky, as the truck pushed me, I started veering all over the place. I crested the hill at the same time I ran off the road and rolled to a stop in a meadow. And then... I woke up.

I'm not a dream analyst. In fact, I usually don't even remember my dreams. But this one seemed particularly prescient considering the content of this book. The uphill battle of unemployment is one that no professional ever really expects or is prepared for. Even when you plan for the worst, and you are able to survive or even do well financially during unemployment, all the other stuff (loss, grief, shame, loneliness, discouragement, etc.) can still be an unexpected and difficult experience. It took me almost a year just to turn my car on and try to head up that hill in the first place!

There is a lot of talk out there about "retraining." Politicians have encouraged this idea since the economic crash of 2008 created such high unemployment rates. The general understanding of "retraining" is that a worker with currently unemployable skills will go to some sort of training program, or return to school, for a certificate or associate degree in a new skill set that will guarantee employment. The thing that many teachers don't realize about themselves, especially when they've been traumatized by the loss of their position, is that they really *are* experts in their field. We don't just have a basic set of skills; we have expertise that is not only valuable to our profession, but also valuable to society at large. Harnessing that expertise and turning it into the fuel that moves us along the new path on which we find ourselves is really the key challenge when we find ourselves off our expected course. "Retraining" may not be the answer for a laid-off teacher. Rather, "re-purposing" might be a more apt description of how to flexibly use our skills.

Focusing only on full time work in the classroom can actually keep us from honing that expertise and working on our professional advancement. Being a teacher is a *lot* of work and most teachers now are exhausted because of the endless mandates they must comply with, the overcrowded classes, the diverse needs of each of their students, and just the basic planning, assessing, and organizing required. When, amidst all of that, do teachers have time to think through and develop their own areas of expertise? The good news is that the every day best practices that you engage in as you educate already enhance your expertise. The real challenge is simply finding time to target what that is and to begin to look for ways to build it for yourself. These are not the days to be completely at the mercy of school districts and schools as funding and resources become scarce. Now is the time to begin to map your own path of expertise, and, as mentioned in Chapter 8, find your personal brand.

Losing my position, no matter how passionate I was about teaching high school social studies, and no matter how much I loved my students, was a wake up call to me about my own professional goals. The path I had been on was comfortable, and I felt secure in not really having to strive for any major changes for myself. And then, when my direction suddenly shifted, I was unprepared to follow a new road. I didn't need retraining into a different career field; I needed to retrain my own mind about how I can use my expertise and skills in the career field I love. Or, to use the analogy in the book title, I didn't want to just give up on the test – I wanted to finish it despite my broken pencil. Realizing that education has so much more room for teachers outside the traditional brick and mortar classroom than I first understood was one of the biggest paradigm shifts I experienced. Now that I have begun to learn how to repurpose my teaching passion and skills, I am not so fearful anymore of the unknown, and I am embracing the idea that I can create my own professional future.

I still may return to a traditional high school classroom (I'm still looking!). But I'm no longer tied to that single path. Because I embraced my own personal goals and expertise, new doors started opening for me. I now teach high school online. I write social studies curriculum and do standards mapping and sequencing. I've done some education advocacy consulting; helping teachers connect with their legislators and advocate for their profession. I am an editor and writer for one of the fastest growing education publications online (*The Educator's Room*). I have submitted proposals to present at several conferences, and I'm attending others. I am teaching small groups of students who are outside the traditional school system, which requires an entirely new kind of planning and teaching. I am completing my second master's degree, and will be qualified to teach at local colleges and other institutions. I went from one form of teaching that didn't really move me anywhere professionally to more opportunities and varieties of education experiences than I could have imagined just a year ago.

No matter where my path leads from here, my new reality is that I will be able to adjust and finish the test. For a teacher who has lost her classroom, been unemployed long-term, and had to learn an entirely new way to think about her own profession, this is a triumph – broken pencils and all.

"The best thing for being sad," replied Merlin, beginning to puff and blow, "is to learn something. That's the only thing that never fails. You may grow old and trembling in your anatomies, you may lie awake at night listening to the disorder of your veins, you may miss your only love, you may see the world about you devastated by evil lunatics, or know your honour trampled in the sewers of baser minds. There is only one thing for it then — to learn. Learn why the world wags and what wags it. That is the only thing which the mind can never exhaust, never alienate, never be tortured by, never fear or distrust, and never dream of regretting. Learning is the only thing for you. Look what a lot of things there are to learn."

— T.H. White, *The Once and Future King*

APPENDICES

1: Frequently Asked Questions at the Time
of a Layoff

2: How Do I Cope With This Transition

3: What Now?
Career Change Checklist

APPENDIX 1

Frequently Asked Questions at the Time of a Layoff·

Why *my* job?[12]

Logical, question! You have the right to ask how the decision was made on who was let go/what positions were eliminated. The RiF process is not easy for any of the parties involved, and it's important you know that all those involved pay very close and precise attention to the process. The thing you must remember: **cutting your position WAS NOT PERSONAL**. YOU were not chosen for layoffs, your *position* was, usually based on the seniority of teachers in the district and what programs/FTE's needed to be cut.[13]

---

[12] *All answers are not district or school specific, so keep in mind your own situation will probably vary from mine.*

[13] *FTE: Full Time Employment — usually refers to the employment hours a district determines it needs*

When I'm speaking with my administrator, can I suggest other employment options in the District?

You certainly can make your administrator aware of your willingness to work as a sub, a part time or job share employee. However, any new position opportunities are the District's purview; the administrator does usually not have the power at that meeting to promise or guarantee any employment option for you. Your district may have a recall list, but you may have to remember to indicate your intentions in writing, so be sure to check your contract or the RiF specifics.

Is it okay to ask for references or recommendation letters?

If you have a good working relationship with one or more of your administrators, it is definitely a good idea to ask for a letter of reference from them and/or from other colleagues. Even if you are put on a recall list, you never know if other opportunities to interview for another job or position may present itself to you, and it is good to be prepared with references.

What about my laptop/other school-provided equipment?

Any school/district-provided equipment must be returned to the district after your last day of work. You can check to see if the equipment is available for purchase by employees, but usually it is leased and must be returned. In preparation for this eventuality, it is smart to obtain an external hard drive to back up all of your work and professional and/or personal files you have on your school computer, so that you can transfer all of your files to your own computer once you return the school's property. Plan time to make sure that you return all school property and electronics at the end of the year or the end of your session with the school.

Who else knows about my termination/job elimination?

Staff layoffs should be handled personally and privately. However, because of the nature of a RiF, and because School Board decisions on program cuts are public knowledge, this may become a very public event for all. Please remember: YOU PERSONALLY ARE NOT BEING FIRED FROM YOUR JOB. This is a district-wide layoff and you personally were not targeted, nor are you to blame, nor should you feel any shame for being laid off or having to move positions. All teachers and staff are going through this together, and your colleagues will want to support you and be there for you, as you will for them. In all the swirling emotions of fear, anger, resentment, rejection, shame and uncertainty, the anchor we can all give each other is the certainty that NONE of these decisions was individual-based, they were budget decisions that end up affecting us all on a very personal level. Reaching out to your colleagues and friends in the district will help you get through the next few months, so don't be afraid to reach out.

What if I start tearing up or crying at the layoff meeting?

That's completely normal and natural. Your administrator feels awful about this situation too. It's just painful all around, and it's okay that those emotions can't be contained sometimes. Take the time you need to recover before leaving the office, your administrator will understand and will be prepared to help in any way possible.

Is there any point in writing down what's said to me in the meeting?

Absolutely. It will help you remember the conversation that can often be lost amidst swirling emotions, it will give you a chance to review later what you discussed in case you have follow up questions, and it will reassure you that you are doing everything you need to do at this point.

Can I have union representation at the meeting?

(Obviously this is only pertinent to districts with unions) This is not a disciplinary meeting (you are not being fired!), so you don't automatically need representation. HOWEVER, if you feel more comfortable with someone in the room with you to take notes for you or just be there to support you, be another set of ears, and generally be on your side – then, YES, call or email your Rep and ask them to attend the meeting with you. Your Reps are ready, willing and prepared to help you in any way that they can.

What practical things can I do once I'm informed of my layoff?

- Remember, you are still with your students until the end of the year, and even though it will be hard sometimes to contain feelings about what is happening around us, they still need us and still need the security and stability of their classrooms. **The most practical thing we can focus on is our teaching and relationships with our students.**

- *****Make sure that you **inform the district in writing** that you want to return if you want to be placed on the recall list (if one exists). You should be provided with the materials to do this when you are informed of a lay off.

- **Make sure you know where your employment file is.** If you don't have one, make one for yourself, that includes your licensing information so that you can stay on top of renewing your license, any Professional Development credits you've collected, all of your contracts, your evaluations, etc. All of that information is important to keep so that you can refer to it whenever you need to in the coming months.

- **Keep a folder or record of all the information you need about unemployment**, your insurance, letters and notices from the district, information about transition workshops, and other notes and plans you make for the end of the year.

- **You may need to think about storage space.** You may have accumulated quite a bit of stuff in your classroom, so think about where you will store it all (if you don't have room in your house, you may want to consider sharing a storage rental space with another teacher).

- **Be sure to inventory any items that belong to the school or district**, and plan for how you will transport your personal possessions.

- **Begin to collect boxes.** Take home things you won't need the rest of the year, so that the job is not so huge and taxing on you when the end of the year comes.

What questions should I ask if I'm told I'll be transferred to another position?

Some possible questions might include:

- What time will I have to set up a new classroom for next year?

- What training will I receive before the next school year starts for my new position?

- What training and/or mentoring will be available throughout next year for me?

APPENDIX 2

How Do I Cope With This Transition?

What is the difference between Change and Transition?

In his book *Managing Transitions – Making the Most Out of Change*, William Bridges says it is usually not the **changes** that cause us problems, but the **transitions**. Change is not the same as Transition: Change is often a situation or an event (our Reduction in Force); Transition is the psychological process that people must go through to come to terms with the new situation.

Each of us is going through transition at a personal level, and there is no one timetable for this process, so we will each handle things differently with different timing.

Am I normal? What are some common reactions to trauma or loss when Change happens?

YES! You are normal! Here are some really common reactions to something like we've all experienced with this RiF, whether your position is affected or one of your colleague's is.

Physical Responses:

- Change in sleep patterns
- Change in appetite
- Shallow, rapid breathing
- Dizziness
- Headaches
- Muscle Tension
- Increased heart rate
- Stomach upset

Emotional Responses:

- Shock or numbness
- Anger toward others involved
- Fear
- Depression
- Guilt/Frustration
- Sadness
- Feeling unsafe or vulnerable
- Loneliness

WHY am I feeling this way?

A Reduction in Force is an event that causes by its very nature a sense of loss, grief and sometimes trauma. If you are feeling yourself going through grieving, or the basic stages of loss – that is normal for those of us who are losing positions we love and for those of us who are losing colleagues that we love working with. It is going to be just as challenging to face this change no matter the lens through which we are viewing the future. Have patience with yourself as you walk through this transition, all those feelings of loss are hard, but are shared and you are not alone.

What are some practical things I can do to manage my emotional stress as I go through this transition?

- Care for yourself by eating well, exercising, and resting when needed. Sometimes stimulants like caffeine and nicotine, or depressants like alcohol, will exacerbate the stress.

- Seek out comfortable, familiar surroundings and avoid spending too much time alone.

- Share your thoughts and feelings with those who are supportive and helpful – don't try to block your feelings, it helps to talk about them.

- Set boundaries with people by letting them know whether you want to t about things or not. Communicate your feelings clearly. Others may know how to respond to you appropriately – let them know wh responses are helpful and which are not.

- If you want to offer comfort, please be aware of what the other pers might need in terms of space and time.

- Give yourself time to recover – the conditions above are short term, focus on short-term goals and the immediate reactions will diminish ov time.

I didn't lose my position, and I feel a little guilty about that, and I'r sad about losing my colleague(s). How do I deal with this?

Survivors' guilt is very common in workforce reductions and is nothing to fe bad about. Anything you feel is authentic and the emotions that come wh you transition through this change are normal. It's okay to talk about ho you're feeling with other colleagues who are remaining – it's good to build support network and to know how you can offer assistance to them and to l them know how they can help you. Mutual understanding and support will l necessary for everyone as we move through the changes in our workplaces, th in some instances will be very distinctive and sometimes uncertain.

Now that I have to continue on with my job for the next ____ months, what do I do next?

Focus on the important things: **Yourself, your family, your students.** Everyone around you is affected by this transition as well, and so remember, while you want to care for them, they want to care for you too. Taking one day at a time and focusing on what is important will help you stay on track. Your family and your students still need your talents and skills, and you still need to take care of yourself. It's okay to simplify your life for a while to focus on these few important things.

I know I wasn't laid off or transferred because of my job performance, but my self-esteem has taken a blow because of this. How can I regain some confidence in myself as a professional?

Again, give yourself a little time to adjust before confronting how you are feeling. Re-establishing your self-confidence and presenting yourself to other people will happen on your own timetable. You are highly respected and admired by your colleagues, your administration and your students. This is when you can start to let go of the past and begin to look forward; you can consider your options or explore new alternatives. This may be a good time to evaluate your own personal goals and direction and open yourself to some new professional energy that you hadn't previously considered. You are incredibly skilled and talented and you have tremendous experience to offer – your self esteem will return with gusto as you realize the positive way you affect your students and your colleagues!

Can I get any professional help?

Yes, and please take advantage of this option for yourself because it can really help you navigate your way through this transition. Your district or school may have an Employee Assistance Plan. This often includes free, private counseling sessions with a mental health specialist. Contact your Human Resources office and ask for EAP assistance. HR should arrange for you to coordinate with the EAP provider using a number that allows you to be identified completely confidentially. If your district doesn't provide an EAP, there are other affordable counseling services in your community that you can take advantage of.

Meanwhile, remember to take time for yourself, talk with friends and colleagues, get help and advice as you need it, and know that you are appreciated and respected for the professional you are and for all you have given your students and this district.

APPENDIX 3

What Now?
Career Change Checklist

Amidst all the emotion and loss when a person is suddenly thrown into unemployment, it sometimes helps to have just a practical to-do list to rely on. I attempt to provide that here. Of course, every person's circumstances and coping mechanisms are different, so what works for me may not work for you. My idea here is simply to provide a quick list of things to remember and consider so that you will be ready to move forward into your next chapter.

Collect Your Employment Records.

Make sure you have all your records of employment from your current position before you leave. If you have to work through to the end of the school year, that gives you time. If you find yourself with only a short notice (like many charter school teachers do), your first priority should be to make sure you square your employment records and have what you need to maintain your license and other requirements for your continued professional viability.

Look up Your State's Unemployment Insurance Process.

Every state works differently. You need to find out (1) if you qualify for unemployment (some districts get around this by putting you on "leave" or requiring you to resign instead of officially laying you off – make sure you know exactly what your status is); (2) how to apply for unemployment insurance; (3) what job finding assistance is offered by your unemployment office. Your initial unemployment insurance will last 26 weeks, so be wise about how your budget your time and your money. In some states, you will be able to get a federal extension, but you need to make sure what the rules are in your own state. You may also need to qualify for your unemployment insurance by providing proof of job seeking each week, so be sure you know what your state requires.

Square Away Your Benefits.

You will most likely have your benefits through the end of the enrollment year (usually sometime around September or October). Your school or district should provide you with information on

COBRA insurance. Be sure to read it thoroughly so you can determine the cost of extending any insurance you may need. The scary thing in the U.S. is that most people have health care insurance only through employment, so when that employment ends, it can be challenging to find affordable insurance. Many areas now provide coop medical offices and other pay-as-you-go services should insurance not be available. Be sure to look into other benefits, such as Medicaid, in case you may qualify.

Keep Your Resume Updated.

Even before you ever face a job loss, you should keep your resume up to date and add new skills, professional development, and other expertise. If you lose your position, there is a possibility you may not get back into a classroom very quickly (then again, you might!). Being ready to show your skills and find other ways to stay in education can be a new avenue that you might not have expected.

Find Storage Space.

You have probably collected a LOT of possessions in your classroom. You need to think practically about making sure you get all of your own things packed and put into storage. It is a very good idea to find some space away from your every day life to keep your school possessions. It's hard enough dealing with the loss of your classroom and all the changes that come with unemployment without having to be reminded of it every day. Don't just pile stuff in your home – create some sort of storage area that will allow you some space from your former classroom.

Talk with Someone.

Your benefit plan most likely provides for counseling services. Before your benefits run out, begin taking advantage of that as soon as you can. If you have never talked with a therapist or counselor, there is nothing to be nervous about or ashamed of. There is no stigma in talking with someone who can offer professional guidance and advice through the roiling emotions of a layoff. There are also counseling services that offer sliding scale fees that make meeting with someone very affordable. Do this for yourself. You need to be able to express and think through your concerns and fears as you face your new employment challenges.

Make Appointments to Get Out of the House.

Get yourself out of the house a few times a week at least. If you find yourself home for longer than you expected as you look for work, you need to make sure you don't trap yourself. It's easy to sink into some depression, or anger, or any other myriad of emotions when all you see are the same walls every day. Join a gym, go to the library, and make appointments to meet friends for happy hour or coffee. Give yourself time to socialize or do non-home or job-finding things so that you have some renewing variety in your life.

Don't Job Hunt Every Day.

Looking for a job can be some of the most draining work a person can do. It's time consuming to try to find positions, and it is important to pace yourself. Yes, there is tremendous competition out there, and you want to present yourself as best as possible to potential employers. That means having carefully crafted online applications, resumes and cover letters ready to go. It also means you may have to navigate through many steps and layers of a job interview process. Being prepared to deal with all of the eventualities means not constantly overwhelming yourself with the process – so take a break, don't job hunt every single day. And treat it like a job itself – take the weekend off sometimes too!

Link Up!

If you haven't already discovered the amazing power of social networking by using its tools as an educator in your classroom, now is the time to get comfortable with it. "Pounding the pavement" and making phone calls are no longer the key methods in job-hunting. Now, it is all about how you can best present yourself as a networked professional. If you don't already have one, create a LinkedIn profile and connect to as many professionals as you can to create a working employment environment. If your Facebook page is not one you'd want a future employer to see, create a second one for your professional life. Twitter is a fantastic way to connect with people who not only share your interests, but also may turn out to be key professional contacts. I've met some incredible educators in all areas of the field through Twitter, and I've learned a lot from entrepreneurs, writers and other self-driven people who know how to use Twitter to connect and promote their own personal brand. Finally, consider creating a website for yourself. A one-stop clearinghouse for all you can offer is a great way to advertise your professional expertise. You can write articles and blog, you can display your CV, work samples, and other parts of a portfolio that will help you promote yourself. Connecting to others across the country and finding new learning communities can make a huge difference in how you approach and manage your career change.

Think Outside the Classroom.

In Chapter 9, I discussed some of the problems that have happened because the education profession doesn't take its professionals seriously. No one ever taught me to think outside the classroom – there was never a conversation before I lost my position about what I could do as a professional educator beyond what I taught my students or did as an extra curricular advisor. In fact, you have tremendous talents, skills and expertise that can translate to numerous professional career fields. Building your resume is only one part of thinking about how to continue as an educator after losing or leaving a classroom. This is why Professional Development is key to expanding your expertise: teaching your peers so they can learn from you is an important piece of building your professional brand. As you consider where you want to go after leaving a classroom, consider that though you may only be familiar with the traditional school teaching of your past, you are actually able to teach adults, train other teachers, coach all kinds of professionals, and use your expertise in multiple ways. If you have written and designed curriculum, a myriad of tech companies and other industries can use your planning and writing skills. If you are an experienced instructor of English Language Learners, there are all kinds of organizations and businesses looking for assistance with immigrant and refugee populations. Trust me, I know how hard it is to think about doing something different than what you have been so passionate about – and you may not have to if you find a new teaching position. But be ready to think of yourself as an education professional whose expertise is valuable far beyond the boundaries of the school and district you have called home for so long. The world is waiting for you!

About the Author

Cari Harris is the Assignment Editor and a writer for *The Educator's Room*. She is also a secondary Social Studies teacher, curriculum writer, and an education advocacy consultant. Cari has been a teacher for over nine years, and has taught every secondary level, in brick & mortar and online environments. Her areas of expertise are Conflict Management, Civic Education and Participation, and Social Sciences & Social Justice curriculum at a secondary and college level. In 2009, she was chosen as a James Madison Fellow, a Congressional Fellowship designed for teachers of Constitution-based history and government. She holds a BA in Conflict Analysis & Resolution, an MA in Teaching, and an MA in Political Science (summer 2013). She is a single mom to her 11-year-old son (and admits to frequently losing to him when they play Settlers of Cataan!).

You can find her on Twitter @teachacari, or online at http://EnlightenedInstruction.com or https://www.facebook.com/FinishingTheTest

Photography by: Madeline Metcalf, Madeline Metcalf Photography (www.MadelineMetcalfPhotography.com)

Made in the USA
Charleston, SC
30 May 2013